**Lauri Robertson's poetry is in full bloom.**
Her latest work, ...& Tremolos, is her most mature, most
profound, and most wide ranging to date. The pleasure
of reading her work is considerable, to be savored slowly,
and lingers long after reading. Pour yourself some tea,
a scotch, or whatever you prefer, then sit back and give
these poems the attention they deserve.
　—Mark Wheeler

**This volume, which Robertson claims** will be
her last, offers biting militancy, exasperation, resignation,
bereavement, and goofiness as a defense against despair
in a jagged world. With urgency, patience and longing for
closure, she offers an at times breathless refrain: What is
a (good) moral life?
　—Barbara DiMauro, author of Not Always Sorrow,
and On This Earth

**Lauri Robertson has been a poet who** uses
narrative gently to convey meaning. In ...& Tremolos she
also uses language to search for meaning, and one realizes
what a beguiling proposition that is. There is sense, and
there is quest. Philosophical and aphoristic, she again
asks language to sing, or can't escape it.
　—Ilaria Pellegrini

ALSO BY LAURI ROBERTSON

*An Æsthetic of Stone*

*In Concert*

*Where Do the Memories Go?*

*Après*

*Ça Existe*

*Revenge*

# ...& Tremolos

## Lauri Robertson

SPUYTEN DUYVIL
*New York City*

ISBN 978-1-963908-78-7

Cover photography by the author: "Civray de Touraine, 2019"

Library of Congress Control Number: 2025936428

for Susan Lewis Duffy

"For whose sake henceforth all his vows be such,
As what he loves may never like too much."
—Ben Jonson, "On My First Son"

# CONTENTS

I

In Concert—Before Byrd     13

In Concert—In the Time of Charles (VII) & Joan (of Arc)     15

In Concert—Couperin, Two Harpsichords     17

In Concert—During a Drought     20

In Concert—1. Chopin, 2. Beethoven     22

In Concert, November 2024     24

Addendum—The Page Turner     27

...& Tremolos     28


II

Still Here     37

Community     38

The University's Day of Service     39

The Psychiatrist Said     40

Money     41

Around the Abbaye     42

O' Israel     44

Mr. Z     46

The News     47

What is *is*...     48

...& Tremolos     49


III

*Permis de Conduire I: Code de la Route*     59

*Permis de Conduire II:* The Examiner     60

Marriage, cont'd #3     61

When Afraid a Poem has Offended Someone     62

That Tree     63

A friend...     65

My Mother     66

The Boy     67

...& Tremolos     68

IV

Birds   79

Summer Solstice   80

Triptych   81

Insomnia Encore   83

Awakening   84

Cat Triplex   85

Foxes   87

Fiat   89

Distraction?   90

So, So   91

...& Tremolos   92


V

Vain (& WS, Son. 29)   105

Dear Judy,   106

Elegy Anon   107

for Arlene   108

Bill said...   109

Assisted Living   110

Halting Parenthetical   112

That Thing About the Body   113

Neurology   114

Dementia 3 (& Elizabeth Cotton)   116

Old to Young   117

Secret Garden Finale   118

January 2025   119

One Wants There To Be...   121

...& Tremolos   122


VI

*Gratuit*

The Bad Boyfriend Poems   133

# I

"In Concert" follows the 2021 volume of the same title,
beginning here on a medieval road.

## In Concert—Before Byrd

It was like marching, or not
wandering without being lost
when wandering was an occupation
before any plague, or in each.

Tribal without a tribe
or when humans belonged
to their own feet, followed them
the regenerating pulse, to another life.

The flute is made of wood.
How can music be made of air?
The singer's larynx is made of flesh.
How can song be made of air?

Howlingly beautiful one horizon
to the next, the lute a magical elbow
turned back on itself turned
back in time, to happiness.

Why would a tenor not know
if he's gentle or fierce, walking
the hard ground, for- and backwards
endlessly.

In the distance the organ transcends.
It cannot walk anywhere, but sits inside
where everyone came to rest, choiceless—
tall pines, stray birds, winnowed breath.

Nearer now, near again
the wanderers rejoin and made a chorus.
They're friends. It helps them remember
to sing.

Entirety.
Every wanderer, every instrument
as if civilization has progressed
twitching the hard ground

with dawning and dusking
moving toward finery, more adjectives
and grace notes, other than carrion
and sand to eat.

Wandering to belief, coveted dreams
wandering now with intention
individual stories of yearning and loss
pipe and drum all at once.

Now our lives as they are, with
music and pauses, distinct harmonies
rage, grief and forgiveness
fear, the sad planet, all.

Should we breathe or hold
our breath, train our voices to rest?

# In Concert—In the time of Charles (VII) & Joan (of Arc)

If we were wandering, where were we going?
Battle cries, or just crying? Marching
to or from the plague: *bubonic*—a word
of bubble and sonic footstep or drums
hoofbeats sighing, whining reeds

the sound of wood crying.
We will keep, we will
keep wandering, joining the day
another day. Each of us playing each
wood and song, wood and siren.

Someone may have a voice
for a love song with wine or
a love song to wine. Yes, she's begun!
Deep angel of the fields, swaying but clear
throat a flute, wine like love, and blood.

*Toot toot toot* like childhood toys.
They *are* toys, a drum that dances
like the moon, fluttering hands upon it.
A kettle rumbles and whistles
and we sing again, warm and clear.

What creates cadence
in the earthborn ear? Hands
that flutter because of the drum?
What do we know of love
or blood?

Wandering but time for play
among all wildflowers at once
swaying to diffusing winds.
We will sing not cry. We will, we
will not cry, will not.

Sing quietly, rising, rising to sleep.
If wandering was all along
needing nothing but the clarity
to know: instrument, wood
child, toy. Some like breathing

and drumming at once.
Sticks for whistling circles
around happiness, wandering
on a wire, a triangle for dinner.
*Chevalier, cloche, sonne.*

# In Concert—Couperin, Two Harpsichords

I doubt there are
100 people here, dripping wet
for all the trouble of hauling
and setting them just so
in a hall too great for them—
that dusty, sheepish sound.
Is that why the audience
is so thin?

But, I like the muted reverie
soft padding against the universe.
Must look up this instrument!
What will the reminiscence be?
Must look up so many things—
common, everyday ignorance.

What does one need to know
and know again
because you've had it wrong?
All or a little wrong—the difference
between a gift and a chore
desire and compulsion.
What is a moral existence
an animal whose fur is soft
if we are not?

S says he dedicated his life
to poetry. I think I understand.
Like some blind seeing-eye dog
I dedicate my poetry

to life. What is a moral life?
Harpsichord, philosopher
sheep-soft wool?

Two rows ahead
is a woman and her son
younger than the usual
antiques of us. Perhaps he's
five, snuggling in her lap.
She holds him and kisses him
whispers to and pats him.
He leans in. Why do I think
he's slightly too old
to be quite so content
quite so possessed?

The harpsichord is soft
but so fluid, deliberate
when so much seems
deeply accidental. I will learn
*pluck not hammer,* ask again
what is a moral existence?

Now mother and boy
have moved to the floor
under a window, perhaps
to see the performers better
or stretch out, and so they
have. And now I think
he's six, at least, and she's
barely more than a teenager.
Strange. Could she be

his sister? Swaying
to the music, playing
with a toy bird, or plane
is it, and a feather.

Dusty, soft notes. Let's
snuggle our way to a moral life.

## In Concert—During a Drought

There is music, Mozart and Schubert.
Attend the reverie. It will come.
The quartet is all women, young, elegant
but not quite, skillful but with grimaces.
*Come to me now* they seem to say.
What a world to enter, slender, with tendrils
making more and more faces, and a jolly one
savoring her violin. I don't like the piece—
rats chasing mice, then too sweet.

Now a pianist, a man, an earthly piano
water falling, saying *I am here.*
*How dare you go if there is music?*
Suddenly a storm then back to breezy
disconnected—*What here, here too, too here*
crescendos again, barely touching
 barely a trinkle, march of raindrops.

Our lives are this simple, this fickle.
This now screaming and buzzing, *interdit.*
Is it always music, vaporous, saying, saying
with nothing to say? Melodious cats.

Take me to sleep melody
but not forever, or maybe forever
or wake in a fine season when we had
fine seasons, when there was meaning
and water. When when when
optimism sang

nothing about water or loss
not even mystery, something gifted
to make the world seem whole
to sleep and wake ignorant of thought
or breathing, of breath, just breathing

to bring us, to us, peace at once
neither crying nor singing, or both
at once. To bring us not together
but alive, tease us and sing us
over and over, starting over and over
violence to somnolence, music
so we can hear the rain
blessed rain.

We're falling, but not too far
like a dove to a crumb
on the ground from a star
sap from a pore that oozes song
in this time we're glad to be alive
to live long, melodious lives
as if music knew the way
or the way out.

# In Concert

## 1. Chopin

Racing dancing throbbing
what virtue in virtuosity?
The gentle and the wolverine.
Nothing can move that fast
except hummingbird wings.
He takes his hands
into the light upon the keys
gleaming, aging hands, the pianist
like the composer, once a child
prodigy. What is prodigious
about prodigy? What
of the bones that warp
to the touch of butterflies.
The memory will not leave them.
The small man was screaming
practically from his deathbed.
From where does
Olympiad flutter come?

2. Beethoven

No one's 'voice' so serious
deliberate. So familiar
magnanimous, none
other, not one other.
The pianist is without
a score, all from the sound
of touch, touch of sound.
Precision beyond what
language isn't, nestled in
memory. Willing to speak
simply, some phrases
confident, then blaze.
How much I miss my father
who loved him so.

## In Concert, November 2024
## Saint-Julien-le-Pauvre—Bach, Mozart, Vivaldi

"The arc of the moral universe is long, but it bends toward justice."
—Martin Luther King, Jr.

Freezing, and I'll be
completely crippled
in this very old, very
very cold church
with crippling seats
named for the poor
a saint of the poor.

Not about God at all
just about the poor
the poor, the poor.
Not about God
about stone. How does
stone stay in the sky
old and cold.

A violin pretends
to make music but
it is crying, the whole
quintet is crying
for what we've failed
every day, to love or save.

The soprano is pretending
song, but she's ripe
with all we've lost

ignorantly, purposefully.
She's trying to cry with
her ample human body
of voice and ancient study.

It's not to make us
remember, to find the fiber
of memory or longing.
It is only
to dumbly mourn.

Why doesn't someone say
*The arc does not bend toward justice.*
Why doesn't some say, *Look*
*at the dusty centuries.*

There is no God
only paintings of God
and many, many palpable
gold leaf and brush
saints that line up like poor
orphans with empty cups.

There's no chaos
that can't ensue.
The revelation is
that it does go on
for now.

They live, they die.
It doesn't matter.
They all destroy

black, white, yellow, brown
worthy as a lost, last song.

Cold, the audience is frozen
and rapt with sorrow
the long arc of sorrow.
Please tell me, hope
alone is not itself the poison.
A body is not enough, only
a violin can truly cry.

I cry
not for the dead
or even the dying
but the useless saints
impotence of music
the silence of stone, end
of the arc.

Not about God—
there is no God—
but the tears of God.

## Addendum: The Page Turner

What page might turn to reveal
a soft thud or siren, harpsichord or violin.
What a job, the page turner!

On stage in full light, dressed as a performer
for no reason. An old woman, once a teacher
once aspiring, once a lover, glad to have

even this, to be inspired by the altar
the spire, statues of saints
dreadful cornucopias in bas relief.

Wipe that timeline of vulgar Baroque!
One can imagine it removed
to stone, the bones of centuries.

There's an older angel, more Medieval
companionable, in the shape of a bird
or a bird in the shape of an angel.

Singing together, the older man
and the younger woman, dancing
animals, not with bodies, exactly

but notes, keys and bows
homage to pagan flight
the page turner's silence.

All day to sit, still as a saint
quietly as an empty hall, waiting.
Only one moment is right.

## ...& TREMOLOS

This is a bleat
and there will be
tremolos.

~

Meant to tweet
but didn't get to it.
Then 'X' came along...

~

≤ 280 characters

quip

aphorism

dictum

adage

epigraph

fragment

~

OK, here you go
OCD ADHD
poetry.

~

Better write it down
before your wisdom tarnishes
or dies of indifference.

~

So many points.
How does anyone
get to the point?

~

A poem is a ripe thing.
It needs to be written
*pronto,* eaten *pronto.*

~

Try aiming for natural speech
unless you're singing.
Then it's a song
remembered from childhood
word for word
or smudging a few.

~

Where are the voices crowded with song?

~

Listening for the voice that found song
or invented it: pure instinct or geometry
a cauldron without sentiment, a dimple
before civilization.

~

(@ Jorie Graham on Emily Dickinson)
Once you hear the voice
it will be coherent, a stream
the river stones embrace
or can't escape.

~

Don't try to write them, try
not to write them. Look
sidelong. They pulse
like oxen on a steep hill.

~

You don't write them. They
write you. And, right you
and wrong you.

~

When the mind works
if it works at all, it works
in vignettes, fragments
surfing the synapses
decades of mush
this brain stuff.

~

Let something new begin
here. Something old.
Vignette your heart out.

~

Stay with me.
If I'm too literal
I'm trying to be.

~

Oh make a virtue of obscurity
*thought, word & deed.*
What if word was spelled
*woord?*
Wouldn't that be weird?

~

Are they orators or oracles?
Drunk on words
or just plain drunk?

~

Dear poet, write lit crit
if you must, but
please don't read it.

~

The purpose of a poem?
To kidnap you.

~

Let me litter you with alliteration.

~

There's cadence first
without words, sometimes
an almost chiming rhyme.
Then you're bluffing
but maybe riffing.
What is form, beloved form?

~

Language is the ghost
of what existed before
and still exists
in ghostly form.

~

Once again, there's word play
because words play.
They're playful. Author-ity!

~

Language begets language.
If memory fails, you're
allowed to make it up.

~

There's no such thing
as 'making it up'. Everything
comes from somewhere
the deeper the better, perhaps:
beneath sinew, within bone
the far wail of marrow.
Even language is unforgiving.

~

OK, I hate imagery. Or, let it be
more zany. Does that say
*move, be?* Yes, it must.
The drive to move and be.

~

Go ahead, make them surprisingly
piquant in their banality.

~

There's a place for trite, sincere
formality. *Dear friend.* Neither
clever nor snide. Hallmarkish
a time for platitudes.
*"...a way of writing I once found heartless."*
    —Robert Lowell

~

Humor comes in odd places.
Silly gooseness, silly gooseitis.

~

Once I used *feckless* in a poem.
Not sure I know what it means now
if I ever did.

~

...a certain kind of much of a muchness
that at a certain point you can say
you've had enough of enoughness.
Try not to let the words get in the way.

~

Things used to be *swell*
then they were *cool*, if not *awesome*.
Now they're *epic*.

~

A tiny little pencil
fits between fingers
like a tiny little sandwich.

~

Something about fonts
how they have faces
and can be like old friends
for different occasions.
More articulate than clothing
they have names.
You don't have to launder them.
There's comfort in particularity
choosing from arrays.
Design is bone
that becomes one's familiar.

# II

"Time wears us old utopians."
—Adrienne Rich

## STILL HERE

The secret garden is still here.
After all, where would it go?
There's new meaning to 'low hanging fruit'—
an apple tree, a fragment with two perfect apples
aligned like testicles, barely two feet tall.

The garden itself has no meaning
no secret at all, except it exists
and we grow old.

There was never a utopia, only the crazy illusion
or longing, and that was enough, even better.
We love anticipation, but now vision
is only the unwanted, unbidden, if gentle
rustling of trees, and the same death.

I've said before I do not like us at all
as a species. I see no relief but great slivers
of joy: party, celebration, repast.
I do not like us but see miracles of stone
yes, Notre Dame, a barn unable to collapse

in the not-so-secret-garden
Western and Eastern hegemonic beauty
beyond God, and God: what, who, whose?

## COMMUNITY

The satisfying swell of self-
congratulation. Strange, they all agree.

At the meeting the usual queens and drones
chime, hush for a mayor, fat cat.

Do all communities have
competitive celebrity connoisseurship?

Of course one wants to be among like-minded:
a place, identity, friends for a long time

the balm of familiarity, gentle or not so much
gossip, commune, communion.

Or the gossip is different now
who's losing it, and who's dead.

Don't leave the room, you'll be
talked about or extra specially unnoticed.

Don't leave the room and return to find
nothing changed in the Petrified Forest.

## THE UNIVERSITY'S DAY OF SERVICE

I read that one option was
lunch with blind Veterans.

Not just veterans, but blind
Veterans. Apparently only

one day of service, though.
Take a day off to plant a tree

or lunch with blind veterans.
What if they see more than you

even without lunch? Did you
bring it? What did you make?

What if they can't see
all the good you do?

## The Psychiatrist Said

I've known them all, every one of them
and they're all alike, and all different.

On the street or mountain top or
in between. I've known their sorrows
rages, raves, cages, ecstasies, pets, regrets.

I've known them drunk, trying to sell
a bouquet at a restaurant door, or stepping
into the restaurant proper, if allowed.

Why is 'people watching' a thing?
Surveying our own kind for costume and caste.
(Yes, follow the teenagers for style.)

But as a pastime? I've known (and loved?)
each and every one of them: anxious student
lonely husband, beleaguered architect's wife.

Regarding *the other,* the homeless addicts
the scent of piss and cigarettes in Paris
I pass each morning, the world and I *othering.*

They always seem to have a dog
or two. No one to blame but we who
blare sirens, fail to imagine the next regret.

I used to think, deep down, we're all alike.
Where is the dog today?

# Money

It means nothing to you
except that you're hoarding it—

keeping from someone's table—
while the billionaire is humbled

before the multi-billionaire.
Let me ask, honestly, what

can you do with it? Another what?
How lonely. Another plane? Are you

at home only in the air? Five star
everything? Isn't the insulation

suffocating? No world except singular
luxury. How bleached, how bland.

I mean it sincerely, another bauble
really? How not in the slightest

there there. Art? Maybe a little, oh
they need patrons. Intellectual?

F'get it. Except when it comes to
making more. Can you even count

that high? More, more, why, why
entire cultures, cultureless for it.

Oh, oh, oh where is reparation
longing only for safety.

## AROUND THE ABBAYE

The old Abbaye is a school.
This is not new. But, now they've filled
the wetlands in with a rugby field.

The town donned a fake fish pond
for real fish, a line of studied trees
where there had been reeds.

The goats and geese are gone.
I saw a juvenile duck recently
but think it was just lost.

Some of the students are from Paris.
Some of them, neither Right nor Left
I've heard are Royalists.

*Liberté, Égalité, Fraternité.*
Off with their heads! The French
indeed know how to cut stone.

The shopfronts are empty, many.
Of course there's a beauty salon
and, thankfully, a boulangerie.

There are tomatoes and potatoes
astonishingly, equally precious.
The French take their potatoes seriously

as they should—incomparable tubers.
There's softness, a lux, tranquility
artful chilis strung across window lace.

Being can be negotiated, up to a point
to belong or not, center or periphery.
Breathing the same air, hearing gossip

even without a common language.
How is that possible? And yet
I know all about people I don't know.

I know the doves, no further rhapsody
and am no longer afraid of bats.
At least the stinging nettle has survived.

## O' ISRAEL

Progressive egalitarian, did I even know
deep down I thought Jews

have a higher moral standard
practically invented ethics?

Not the Hassidim. They don't
live in this world.

Nor the Sacklers. Maybe they were
poisoned by their own drugs.

O' Israel!
Where I was briefly a peripheral Jew.

Where I hugged Golda.
All her good? Not now

not with blood on your face
our even 'just ethnic' hands.

As it is said:
When the apple wears the honey—

I was always shocked by the plagues
how violent they are

how we wished them on anyone—
"Egyptians" whom we know—

even in barbaric times
even in the desert.

O' Israel
I leave you

all your irrigation
all my ignorance

and you leave me
with blood at my feet.

## MR. Z

Today I read
he's willing to step down
for a certain *d'accord.*

Can you begin to imagine
how tired this man must be?

Wondering, perhaps, what's
worth dying for, or
living...a generation dead
at the hands
that tied his hands.

Don't they know
the post-truth universe
is too small for gang wars?

Perhaps a way out
still alive, to sit and
grow old, grow
vegetables.

Where he could go
to a simple life
in the countryside, or complex
with sojourners and treatises.

He still looked
improbably well though
though had lost
more than even history
will be able
to figure out.

## THE NEWS

So many beautiful objects
we've made and thrown away, brass
and glass, crystal and blown, wood
revered, and stone.

They all seem unimportant now, utterly.
What could be in this world
of ceaseless crisis? The decrements
that take life, and take it, and take it

as if it were not all going
to be taken away, anyway.

These hours are for looking
through the branches of gauzy trees
gauze of fortitude, those trees willing
to live with us, after all we've done

willing to live
unwilling not to.

# WHAT IS *IS*...

> "Time wears us old utopians."
> —Adrienne Rich

Yes, it does, down
to the nub, the cave below
sea level, where all of Venice
will sing with the fishes.

Old, I said I'd say
no more about watching death
from the chiming years'
chimney tops. But

take it, take in your hand
the last value, the last apology:
ambition, craft, hope, children.
Let me ask again *again;*

What is *is* a good moral life?

## ...& Tremolos

Is this wave a sea change?

~

How can a person be 'illegal'?
How can my personhood not *be?*
My body be. *A body in motion*
*stays in motion.*

~

New York, inoculated or imprinted
(or that psychoanalytic word, *introjected)*
comfort in this oasis of stink.
Once a NYer, always a NYer.
What separates the haves
from the have nots
is not the having
but the *not.*

~

All this work to stay alive
fed and clothed
to not be a murderer
then someone comes, naked
abstract, invisible
to murder you.

~

Why do we love
the sordid and sensational?
Why do I feel
*The NYT* is *The National Enquirer*
of my childhood?

~

Such a mean-spirited thing
happened to the USA.
Maybe we deserved it.

~

The audacity of sociopathy.

~

The irony of success is what
you then have to dispose of.

~

Have grave questions
about what you aspire to.

~

All like cats, individuals
but the same species.
All with ambition to belong.
All ambition is fallacious
or immoral.

~

From a major health educator:
"From Our Family to Yours—
Have a Wonderful & Safe Holiday ☺
and buy our online course."

~

I never wanted to be rich
I only wanted to be *safe*
whatever that means.
Now unsafe as ever
death watching every
saved, polished penny.
Spend it, dammit!

~

In a major medical journal:
"Return on Investment
of Enhanced Behavioral
Health Services"

~

Buying the Magna Carta
starts to seem more
like a lack of imagination
than status.

~

"Isn't it hard to have Asian parents
who want you to study all the time?
American parents just want us to be happy."
"Well, it's easier to study than be happy."

~

In the village every inch is beautiful:
wisteria, hair, rain, tears falling.
Aristocrats are our friends.
We hear sometimes the homeless
live as squatters in the old abattoir.

~

Art:
No actual value. You can't
eat it or sleep on it (usually).
Not much purpose at all
if you're blind.
But, it's helped us cry
for centuries, feel how
trite we really are
how unfailingly episodic.

Stone carved to our desire
will not remake the first embrace.

~

Paris:
A lot of new buildings
are built to look like
they're falling down.

Wiggly or astigmatic.
Abstract and artful.
Bloated or shrunken.

But, not like in cities
that are actually
falling down.

~

Silly, fussy overpriced food.
Sorry, someone has to say this.
Paris, but not just Paris.
Foam. Why is that a good idea?
Like detergent washing up
in the corner of a pond
or certain deadly algae blooms.
We want real food. Can there be
flavor without tweezers?

~

*Primum non nocere.*
The Hippocratic Oath
should apply to more
apply to all and
all we do.

~

*for* Gregory Pardlo
What concerns you, this.
This that burns your heart
at any moment. Always
and long ago. But, this
moment.
When everyone is lost
in their own moments
unto starvation or death.
Or history seems
unbelievable. Believe it
and weep. I mean it.

~

On the *tsuris* of the world—
What is it that wants to devour itself?
Cobwebs hang like daggers.
This has happened before
long ago, and not so long ago.

~

A bishop
asking for mercy
is spat on by a toad.
Like asking fire
not to burn, begging
wind to subside.
The civilized pay
because they
cannot draw blood.
Because we have only words:
*I hope your unvaccinated corpse*
*lies in a refrigerated truck*
*in Elmhurst.*

~

Something to be said
about truth.
We grew up on it
the good of it:
George Washington
confessing he cut down
the cherry tree, your own
integrity, which may be
all you have.
Sometimes complicated
but different
than a lie.

~

There used to be
good guys & bad guys.
Now there
are bad guys
and bad guys
and worse guys.

~

I am weeping for the Partisans in the forest.
They had signals, signifiers. Someone I knew
told me before she died, before living memory died.
There were secrets and ways, but you had to consider
to remember, never forget the apocalyptic danger.

~

The trees endure, on the margins
or free within the last virgin forest.
I know what I cannot endure.
Sometimes it's time
for the atheist's serenity prayer.

~

Let God
Jehovah, Allah, Yahweh
for a little start
pick them all up
by the scruffs of their necks
and say, *Stop!*
Murder, war, oppression, disgrace.
Let my children
play nice
(and not breed so much).

III

## Permis de Conduire I: Code de la Route

### The Triumph of Pig Latin

I passed the famously difficult *examen écrit*
for a French driver's license
in French. But, I don't speak French.
...studied my little taillights off
still dreaming of *giratoires* and *clignotants*.

Equal parts relief and feather fluffin'
sumpthin'. And not to be jailed
for illegal rides to the grocery store
swerving to avoid excruciating, possibly
irreparable narcissistic injury.

Mostly I try
to 'maintain my allure'.

Well, there was once a German exam
but I don't speak German. OK
it was chemistry. They gave us a recipe
and let us use a dictionary. Ha!
I passed. And, now it's a family joke

my 2nd language is Pig Latin.
Somewhere between swindle, swine and what
used to be known as 'deep structure'
language has saved me. I hear there were
'linguistic wars', a word better than a sword.

Linguistic swords. *Igpay Atinlay.*

## Permis de Conduire II:
## The Examiner

| | |
|---|---|
| Rude | *Grossier* |
| Unpleasant | *Désagréable* |
| Hostile | *Hostile* |
| Contemptuous | *Méprisant* |
| Intimidating | *Intimidant* |
| Humiliating | *Humiliant* |
| Sadistic | *Sadique* |
| Bastard | *Bâtard* |
| Pathetic | *Pathétique* |

You're not allowed to shoot or stab. (*Aucune violence armée en France!*) But, wish a big fat cardiac attack on his puny heart. Or, how about a vicious stray dog ripping a bit? Unlucky in love? Retired Gestapo? Pension (or putz) not big enough? Do you hate foreigners? Will you take a bribe (and go to jail)? Do you hate women? Do I remind you of your mother who cursed your birth? Do you hate your life? Do you beat your wife? Or just torture her psyche? Or, no woman will come near you? Do you hate old people? I am an old, foreign woman. Was it necessary? Do I hate you? I do. *Oui.*

I do. I do. *Oui. Oui.*

I do. *Oui.*

# Marriage, Cont'd #3
## Pissed

Precocious in my worry, yes.
Or maybe I'm just enraged with you
and wish you dead.

Then it would be fruitless
to let you know how angry I am.
Now I can just monosyllable you to death.

I can give you what you wish for:
freedom, all the junk food available
in Paris, and there's a lot.

Withholding the modest delights
of home cooking for coronary sauce.
"Where are you taking me tonight?"

Showing you the pleasures
of a vacuum cleaner, and the unethical joy
of trying to find a *femme de ménage*

who will not steal your fucking silver
or unwittingly destroy your precious
comfortless brown furniture

while I condemn you for failing
to clean your own toilet
and everything else.

# WHEN AFRAID A POEM HAS OFFENDED SOMEONE

"If people wanted to you write more warmly about
them they should have behaved better."

—Anne Lamott

Look, it ain't journalism
(or what journalism should/used to be).
It's about some kind of emotional reality
to someone somewhere sometime.

And, it has many shades
and contradictions, often morphing
into one another.

The answer here is: *Grow some*
as the (sexist) saying goes.
Just say, *I'm civil, I'm appropriate.*
How guilty can I be?

From a lovely story @ Japanese students:
*What unforgiving instruments we are.*

## THAT TREE

The thing about that tree—
Did you think there was
no myth there? Of a broken limb
roof's edge, the last leaves that fell
like musical notes without a sound.

It was music that begat music
not contagious, but stirring.
That literal tree started everything
blowing. Then fictions became
swarms of extinct animals. Became
emotion and religion.

Dry, I began reading, a book
on the shelf for a while
by a famous, now dead poet
I felt a snarl for. So, happy
to find I didn't find it all that good
or very good at all, and that he—
poet/persona/person—seemed
someone I disliked all the more.

That, not the nicest sentiment
was a spark. Suddenly words
began to dance phrases, taunts.
The power of what poetry is
however much I cherish the literal.
Make it up, and it'll be no more
fantasy than a room you enter
and are forced to live in.

Cherish the dull beyond the extravagant
but the latter can take you home.

The poem about the tree
is literal. It says what it means
and means what it says
A tree is faithful 100%.
(Childhood just sprung that!)
And, the myth isn't even
in the recrimination or lesson
metaphor, personification or sadism.
It's in the branches, pith and phloem
the feeling for something so trivial
the conversation with the inanimate
that had no reason to occur.

# A friend...

...from years and years ago seems to have
changed her style to a strange, foreign flare.
But, we've met again, on Facebook, and she is ill.
My heart goes out to her in a certain, indescribable way:
to say you have an old friend, deep and slight
as you're leaving the planet. To say this moment
is without a future, just let it float, or caress
so lightly there's no awareness of touch.

It's a style I neither recognize nor like—
garish and motley, overly tinseled and rouged.
Puffed and poofed. But, have I changed mirrors too?
*Au natural* gone funereal? Teeth gone yellow, of course.
I'm glad both she and I have had better lives than imagined.
We both hated our mothers. Not, maybe, hated, but
each was dreadful beyond teenage complaint.
I don't know what she thinks now.

She cooks a lot, and is 'motherly' to all in her good will.

# My Mother

She wasn't even a person
or was, in my imagination.

My father's words: *You will never
know her as I did.*

I searched for her, and searched.
She existed in photographs.

I created her, over and over.
*You will never know her as she was.*

Childlike and *marginal*
even the analyst said.

But, she was kind and
generous in a childlike way.

Some curled in her lap
injured or sad, but never I.

Though once, when I was
in bed with an ear infection

she read to me, *Black Beauty*.
I cried when Ginger

the horse stumbled.

## THE BOY...

...didn't want
to talk to his father
who didn't know why.
I call him a boy because
that's what he was
then.

His father is not
a bad guy.

The ghosting went on and off
off and on, then on and on and on.
Hope became something
like a reflex to rhyme.

*Why, boy, guy, rhyme.*
Or slant rhyme.
On and on, *chime, chime.*
What *time*
is it?

Is it too late?
What is he (which he)
waiting for?

## ...& TREMOLOS

Certain things
must let fade
without rumination
recrimination
with a little sadness.
Perhaps an old friend isn't
who you thought they were.

~

There's a quality of self-importance
she gives to trivia. Yet my own
is revelatory.

~

We were all living in Paris
with our desires fulfilled or un...
The young woman is tall
almost beautiful, trying too hard.
What is desire? To be what one sees?
Why are we all
trying too hard?

~

Heard on the street: "Actually
I step out of my comfort zone
habitually, then long
to go back in."

~

I cannot imagine being blind
having to touch the world, literally.

~

The lives you don't live
live you, an illusion
of volition entirely.

~

No confidence
it will be any good
but now the courage
(or arrogance)
to do it.

~

Wasn't I told
to let my hair down?
Little did they know
it was all effort
to contain Medusa.

~

What delusion were you chasing
in that man, birthed like a racehorse
by desperation, out of despair?

~

Anticipation larger than
the hope of sight, greater
than the population of India.
Will you be robust and ecstatic?

~

No dress rehearsal:
How happy or sad is how you'll be
how lonely or pensive, social or proud
in that moment after time passes.

~

Destiny found for you—
intrinsic, inexorable
the reticence, the snarl—as if
it could be otherwise.

~

Their fates wore on me—
that one or the other's
would be my own.
Now decades away, I was the
Phoenix supposed to fly
out of the ashes
and did. Oh, that gets
wearying, too.

~

My mother liked to chew ice.
It drove my father crazy. Now
I find it so normal, the crunch.

~

She'll become the old woman
who cooks for you, desire worn
corporeal to ethereal.

~

What holds your heart's desire
is all, however transient or
shallow the refuge. What you
cannot touch—too cold or hungry—
touches you. So much to love, then
the anathema of Armageddon.

~

It was a birthday lunch
and we wept, real, crazy old
tears of joy. And, I do mean *old*.
...to have picked
the burrs from our fur
and kept the champagne
rare.

~

Make peace, make peace.
Make the best
peace you can.

~

The signal for discomfort
or regret doesn't come
until it's too late.

~

Indeed, higher quality suffering
gets better ethical grades.
(Did you know there's no
such thing as WASP guilt?)

~

Yes, I love The French.
They're crazy, know how to
chop the heads off saints.
Brits just make me feel
sniffed at.

~

I am sorry if I'm not
decorous enough for you.
I did not come here to meet
your approval. You are not
nice enough for me
(or smart enough).

~

Life of the mind:
Actually, the mindless.
I don't mind, but please
remind me. Presence
of mind. Never mind.

~

Toni Morrison makes me cry
every word, inside and out. Why?
Not because she writes of sorrow
but because she holds her head high.

~

Yes, please tell us *the source*
and we'll drink from it, as if
from the fountain of youth.

~

Don't tell me anything.
Just give me longing
the scent, Neolithic.

~

A thread of meaning, a thread of desire
a thread of memory. What comes to you
within the quiet familiar?

~

Sorrow of ages
sorrow of now
sorrows unknown
of the unknown.

~

He stopped speaking
not to everyone.

~

She hadn't known him
but could tell he'd been here.
Apparitions are like that
pure and clear, a scent
everywhere she searched.
Was it of her brother or
an intruder, for love or $.

~

Dig me with a trowel.
Dry me with a towel.

~

You were going to spread your wings.
What do they look like? Do they
have feathers or are they steel?
Fly? How trite.

~

Who ever thought an atheist Jew
would be praying for the Pope?

~

Just need to be here
to search the days through days
drip of desire, drip of rain
felicitous purposelessness.
Cook very simply.

~

Wherever you go, there are you
truly patchouli, escaping neither
guilt nor shame. The truth
silhouettes itself helplessly.
Contradictions matter
less and less.

~

We live our fantasies or love them.
(Which was written down?)
No matter, each is true.
Even the happiest couple
asleep side by side, holding hands
invent each other.

~

Thinking of what everyone else had
that I didn't. It wasn't bitterness.
It was hunger.

~

My mother had a certain gift
for making the do-gooders
feel good
and do all the more good
especially for her.

~

She mourned an empty womb
but, truth is, she wanted
the mother she didn't have
more than she wanted
to be a mother. The same
was true for me. Generations
of motherless daughters
no more.

~

My cousin said simply
"I know my limitations."

~

To the analyst: "So, Dr. Katz
did you have nice parents?"
He answered with words I've repeated
to many, wisdom beyond fortune.
*I may not have thought so at the time.*

~

As a little boy
he loved fishing.
He could stand all day
at the edge of the stream
that ran behind his house
or the pond they drove to
on weekends. His father made
a special hook, with no hook.
He was never in danger
of catching anything
or being caught.

IV

# Birds

And, they cackle and hum, squawk.
After all, they're only birds
doing what birds do, fly.

South now, or intercontinental.
They know the way, the time.
But, apprehension. Something's
changed. The season, of course.
We all know. And, it means, what?
Melancholy? Delight? All
lovely but, hold still the world
please hold still, still, please
hold.

They're our birds, you know, *birds*
just birds, as we've always known.
Haven't you noticed them?

## SUMMER SOLSTICE

Brighter than bright
still about the light
diminishing each brilliant day.
So summery and so sad.
Not quite yet, but knowing
and that the dazzle will turn
*au coeur de l'hiver.*

No, don't go!
Though the birds chime before five
and only old people go to bed lit.
Light of my life!
It's direction that matters.
We'll have wait until December
to be happy again

needing the glow
to see what disaster
will befall us next.

# TRIPTYCH

Oh so lovely here if the mood is right.
Spangled afternoons, blinking trees
with nothing to do. Watching the minutes
wasting themselves. Is that the same as
not having a life? As if all memories
have been remembered and archived.

\*

I could sit here, old glass
making the world wavy
for a long time. More so
if you move your head
up and down, like saying
*yes*, and especially, from
side to side, like saying *no*.
I could sit here, perched
like a bird, without thoughts
looking out for a long time
at the thoughtless, wavy world.

\*

So nice, this world. No, not
*the* world, this little world.
Even as the season dies down
in slanting light, too lush to survive.

There's the curvature of the staircase
to notice, the spindles awkward, warped
with age, and the stairs themselves.
They led somewhere once, still do

if you dare to climb, like the crazy roses do
all over the place. But, the second bloom
is almost nothing this year. *Rien à faire.*
My atheist god doesn't want you here.

## INSOMNIA ENCORE

Falling asleep. Why is it
*falling?* Into what, where?
An elusive darkness away
from the bright moon face
longed if not begged for.
So simple, often inescapable.
I beg you, Morpheus!
No worth in consciousness.
Let it go, fall, fall, fall down
to the bay of distant hounds
before the crazy early dawn
and damn birdsong.

Why *do* they call it falling?
Why not rising
to the darkness above?
A different infinity.
Rising asleep. I thought
I might never wake.
I thought these sensations
may be the last and
unmemorable. Why not
rising to oblivion
an alternate universe
our shared fragments
created *seriatim.*

## Awakening

I used to curse the birds
because they woke me prematurely.
Now I thank them for being willing
to live among us with our steel and glass
ambition poisoning their nests.
Now I listen to songs I'd never heard
call and response, as in a church
I'd never been to. (I've never been
to any church.) Celebrate their bird-like
determination, feathers against the rain
air as habitat, music for what was cursed.
No awakening is premature.

## Cat Triplex

Fritz has had a terrific run
of luck, that cat has. It helps
to be lucky with your luck.
You see, he was quite the bully
but someone saw the light in him.
Someone said they thought
he was just misunderstood
then cut his balls off.
(Luck has many faces.)
But, it helped, along with
a warm bed, a warm lap
and a lot of supper.
He stopped terrorizing
the entire neighborhood
(mostly). It helps to keep
your luck lucky.

*

*Whispering to Charlemagne.*
*Hi Charlie, Sharlee, Sharles*
*Buttons, Puppy. You're*
*a cat. Did you know you are*
*a cat? How long have you*
*been a cat? Have you always*
*been a cat? And then, he wasn't.*
Surprise and certainty outlasting
and a legacy coronation.

\*

Gisèle, not the ballerina
was King Charlemagne's
astronomer daughter.
*Hi G, Gigi, Goose, Goo*
*Goo-goo, Guh'goo.*

## FOXES

*The fox went out on a chilly night...*
—Traditional Folk Song

I refuse to romanticize them
as others have, or anything else.
Neither lyric nor image

haiku or sonnet.
Poetry dies in its own bed.
But, I love them

their beautiful triangular faces
Moulin Rouge stockings
and bat ears.

I love them like dear friends
but with an intimacy as if our lives
and eyes were superimposed.

I had a dog once, named *Fox*
because he resembled one
especially when his legs

were black with mud. A dog
who ran away from his apparently
perfectly nice family, I learned

downtown one day, when someone
called, "Buffy, Buffy". He greeted them
happily, then returned to me.

It was many years ago
but how that love
squeals now, refusing poetry.

How old does one have to be
to ache for the uncelebrated past?
If only all my dead beloveds

would simply return, unadorned
as they do in dreams sometimes
and yours, too.

Did you know Dmitry Belyayev
made them friendlier, perhaps
friendlier than they wanted to be?

# FIAT

You have to
slow yourself down.
What did you want?
Success and survival
(necessarily not in that order).
Down to the birds singing
in the countryside
the *nothing there* countryside.
(Good, keeps interlopers away.)
Ambition fades on its own.
(What contempt we had
for the young with none.)
Slow to the whispers.
Still fast enough to flick an ant.
Slow, but here's a venture—
gift everything you have.

# DISTRACTION?

A little distraction.
Good for the soul? What soul?
Distraction from questions.
What's a moral life, anyway?
Should I eat a bird? Should I
kill my neighbor? What's 'morality'
anyway? In what context, vein?
Is even language anyone's virtue?
What is natural? *Naturelle?*
Whose language? What names?
I love the wild carrot
a lot like Queen Anne's lace.
But, beware the similarly pretty giant
hogweed. Allergic? Phytophoto-
sensitive? Why is it we don't
know what to love? Or do
until we don't, or do again?
What is a moral life?

## So, So

The moss is green. Oh so, so green.
Iridescent green. Are we on Mars?
Or, are we, ourselves the Martians?

Behind the leafless winter trees
is a straggly pine. But, oh so tall.
So, so tall. Is it only old people

who think it's the end of time?
Or, think backwards in time
to those bad times, so, so bad

overflowing with iridescent hatred
and not enough planetary tears
to drown the flames.

## ...& Tremolos

Even less 'intentionality' here.
The flowers have names, but just exist
unable to capture movement and noise
birds bees butterflies all at once
wind and fragrance, *parfum*.
Whatever can flutter does.
I've arrived in some heaven
but with tears.

~

The beauty of the world
sustained only by a buzz
of manic refrain?
Trope alone?

~

What will you love next?
Taos.
Nantucket.
France.
Japan.
Novelty.

~

Nothing
was ever as good again
as the French fry a 6th grader
(who was allowed
to leave the schoolyard)
gave a 4th grader from those
bought down the street
in a little paper cone
for 25¢.

~

There's a great lust
to foraging, something for nothing
(though competition with birds):
blackberries near the parking lot
a beach plum whisky sour
mulberry-stained childhood.

~

So you've been seeking out
beautiful places. So what?
Your beach is a momentary
piece of driftwood. Others
live there, with animals
and their skulls.

~

*Should we have stayed at home
and thought of here?*—Elizabeth Bishop
One poet's line, like a mantra
worth all the tea in China.
Home here, dumb & blind.

~

This strange
circling the wagons
you do like a dog
about to lie down.

~

Nantucket & Paris
famous places where
belonging is illusion
or allusion.

~

About something, anything
other than longing
not knowing
for what.

~

What will your eyes see
as they glaze into the distance?

~

Someone has the authority, the answers
to put your mind at rest, console
at least make you feel human again.
A respectful moment, award or reward
revivification of confidence, competence.
A kindness does not do justice
but can unbury the blade.

~

In France the lockdown
was called *confinement*
as in Victorian pregnancy.
But, I like to think *confiture*
beautiful jams one might
have made while confined.

~

The problem with tightening
the little tiny screw on your glasses.
Well, it should be obvious.

~

At the mercy of a different kind of weather:
more fickle, less attended to. Endless motion
of butterflies, humming birds the size of hazelnuts
and dizzying scent. Crickets hastened by wind.

~

A full-throated song or season.
The grapes hang heavier
than geriatric breasts.
Bacchanal treats.

~

What I've learned living in France;
few things are not better with
white wine, and butter.

~

It wasn't a bit of mold
in the wandering eye
of that tomato. It was
a piece of lettuce
because once it belonged
to a salad.

~

Did you know that 90%
of lizards lay eggs, and 10%
have live birth? Isn't that
extraordinary?

~

By a beautiful stream
and your own tears
bore you to tears.

~

Jackdaw *réseau:*
They're tending
those birds are
dipping like buoys
in the November wind.
There are two.
Do they love each other?
Of course they do.
How do I know
in our ignorant
arrogant lexicon?

~

I used to curse the birds
for waking me. I no longer
curse the birds, and don't
know why. I used to curse
the noisy birds, but now they sing
safe from the cat beside me.

~

Death of the old cat lady:
I became her, had been
becoming for years—
a crazy old cat lady-in-waiting.
Please leave out "crazy".

~

A Cat's Life:
A snack and a snooze
and a butterfly.
A shin buff, a shimmy
up a tree. A purr and

*who's paying attention*
*to me?* A stretch and
a scratch. A disobedience.
A snack and a snooze.

"      "      "    "    "

"      "      "    "    "

"      "      "    "    "

~

Tuxedo cat; our masks
of obfuscation or perfection
are over.

~

In the distance, fragments
of a conversation
between a divorced couple.
It sounds neither
happy nor sad, just
  actual.

~

Why marriages come apart;
tolerance is grievance in abeyance.

~

Self-defense, or offense?
Self-offense?

~

A new friend's mother: "Oh, what side
of Metropolitan Avenue are you on?"
"Oh, you wouldn't have heard of us."

~

The old woman, older than I
is selling her house.
Her house her house her house
of a thousand *objects d'art*.

~

We've always had
beautiful rooms
no one sits in.

~

Is it a sanctuary or
is it a prison? (Be careful
your sanctuary doesn't
become your prison.)

~

Don't blame those millennials
for not wanting 'brown furniture'.
Antiques that survived
the Industrial Revolution
die in their hands like
mid-century morning glories.

~

Life in the slow lane:
Made a new label for our
elderly neighbor's mailbox.
Thought about the font
for a long time.

~

Wanting to live in a world
of small concerns, the curtains
are an inch too short, though
the fluting, especially through
the last light of day
is lovely.

~

The curtain is gauzy
or the world is or
mine eyes have seen the glory
of the coming of the fog.

~

A universe kind as apples
small as bread.

~

The little 1920's structure hadn't
been touched since—the shower
authentic white subway tiles
crazed as in a 19th century
psychiatric hospital.

~

...bits of crazy, beautiful light
in the beautiful fireplace
I refuse to use because
I'm afraid of fire.

~

I will sit and wait
until the beauty of the world
comes back to me.

~

These hours it takes
to unbraid my hair.

~

And, the weather is gentle
and the light is gentle.
What could not be gentle
after a 'grayer than the Gray Lady'
winter? What thought could
not have succumbed to...
what? Time passing, oblivion.
What gesture, jester confuses
any thought, or finds it
unworthy?

~

Here (& Masefield).
What have we done for joy here?
We sit in the woods with the trees.
We scream and cry, just to hear
what sounds are human
"...and may not be denied."
(They made us memorize...)
Once you see what can't be un...
you know you can't unknow.
Any dive into history is lethal.

~

Wood, another even more forgiving
act of nature (than stone). Light falling
across it, medieval, and why so imbued
with what has been needed to be
recorded for centuries? What outlasts?
What sat long before, humbly
our good better best efforts
fly speck, flea dirt, absurd?

# V

"When I consider how my light is spent..."
—John Milton

## Vain (& WS, Son. 29)

Why is it that when I was young
I looked like my father, cherub-faced
with a bit of a ball at the end of my nose?
Fred Flintstone legs. It was my mother
who had elegant gams, and a Garboesque flair.
Then she aged into a rather homely pout
*that then I scorned to change my state...*
no, my face, that then I got.

## DEAR JUDY,

But the dead can't read. And you are dead
half a century dead. We were 22
and now I'm 72. You missed
a lot.

The note next to a wire in a tin shed said:
"I decided this morning I do not want to live
a small, crippled life."

And, so you did not.
Nor any. I've had all these extra decades
and cherish them all, cherish the cherishing
even more, and more and more.

## Elegy Anon

The sad journey he made, lumbering.
I didn't know him, others I know knew
but, he is all of us, every morsel of grief
we forgot to feel, or forget every day
because there is no need. He is entirely
anonymous to me, except for the vague
recognition of a name. He is where
we put love when there's nowhere else
to put it. Love of sorrow—strange?
Or something to melt to the core
melt the core itself. Poignant? Raw?
Something remembered from long ago
outlived but sheltered, almost glazed
by sorrow. A near stranger is dead and
another, and another. The anonymous, too.
Why grieve mere lifetimes hurtling
toward their rightful ends?

## FOR ARLENE

You need her
to be in that box
so you can talk to her.

But, she is not in the box.
She's not in the dust
in the box. She is not
the dust in the box.

But, please
do not stop talking to her—
the sound that stirs the ash.
Take everything
she can give you now.

## Bill Said...

...he was unsentimental
about his own death, the prospect.
Well, he was in his 90's. He said
"The end is never pretty."
And, so it was pretty enough—
never needed that downstairs shower
he'd had put in. Woke once
in the hospital, cheerful.

And so I think I feel the same
lack of sentiment about my own
though have lavished on others
including Bill, blinking tears and fear
a certain sauce of sentiment
that's enlivened life, more tender
than morbid, sorrow as solace
that cannot be mocked.

But, the prospect of my own
however unwanted, once at hand
the inevitable if in clear view—
please forgive the brief goodbyes.
I'm looking to vanish in an instant
like thousands in earthquake rubble
the tremor of a hand or a continent
at the end of choice.

## ASSISTED LIVING

Yes, assist me
with living!

This kind of family is normal for me:
summer camp or college, the orphanage.

Be careful what you wish for
wishing for parents (or children).

There may be loving custodians here, some
checks and balances on everyone's madness.

Your own room if you want it, snug.
Yours to decorate, like a little craft project

to hide beneath the covers within or emerge from
looking for random companionship.

They feed you daily, all you can eat, not always bad.
(Though Lily yelped, "Tilapia! What is *that?*)

Never a meal far away, or a face. Practically a city
warehousing the mass affluent.

Bill sneered, "Those places are just a waiting room
for the grave." And, so they may be. Likely.

But, I want to be with my own kind, the wise
not the young with their silly, pointless lives.

The philosophers of Eden, the old and the dying.
Those with time to schmooze, dull as some may be.

I want to live if living is possible, to a standard
TBA, churned and revised.

# HALTING PARENTHETICAL

What are you trying to say?
That your body hurts
the eye, the ear, the tooth
all on the same side.

That they're trying to
make you take the test
over and over and over
until you fail.

That you're afraid
of what? That body or
no time to tell the story
of the last ghost

or ride the wild horses
before osteoporsis.

## The Thing About that Body

You notice when it goes awry
or don't, akimbo unto
someone else commenting
or your own somber realization
too late.

That blotch, that droop.
Lump and lisp.
Walking into walls, wobble.
Lost words or those
that don't make sense.

No, not a list! Yes, a list
*the organ recital.*
Five dollars in the kitty
for every complaint.
Then we'll all go on a trip.

All it takes is a thumb & finger
a wrist on the other hand
to drop the groceries
spill the champagne, now
you're old enough to celebrate.

You don't expect it, you just don't.
You accept it. You just do.
Moving slowly with rubber soles
agility a foreign country
the 'for granted' now an inventory.

# NEUROLOGY

Dearest, the wheelchair is for you
to wheel around the universe.

This is neurology, where
nerve meets muscle (or doesn't).

Where we run in our imaginations
sip with help, limp and drool.

A body needs many things
to leap and sing.

This is neurology, the brain
and the spindles that touch the toes

we hope, the mind as if it's
a thing entire, sentient, even religious

wheeling through history, as if
consciousness was not a fading artifact.

Many of us will land here
and believe it's a planet.

Yes, *this* is neurology
the decade beyond hips and knees

the brain, burning too brightly
or not at all, gaits galore, malaprops.

What did you expect, where there's
no balance, nothing balances, especially

not you.

# Dementia 3 (& Elizabeth Cotten)

You don't have to talk about it
because you will arrive—

*Freight train, freight train...*

That particular way of staring
into nothing.

A hand patting
mostly the air.

That person
whom you knew.

*Freight train, freight train, run so fast*
*Please don't tell what train I'm on...*

You don't have to think about it
or can't.

## OLD TO YOUNG

We say goodbye to one. We say
good riddance (politely) to another.
We say, we say. We're having our say
or have had our say.

We look stupid to you
but the sorry is not stupid. You
look stupid to us, and are, wasting
what, your lives(!) on what?

I know a lot of old folks
cynically, sadly, heartbreakingly
say they hope global warming
will cure you. Of what?

War? Politics? Plastic? We're
the invasive species, anyway. I say
goodbye to the beauty, the capacity
for love, to my silly love

for cat videos, cats, vulnerability to
ads for devices, cheap fashion
(that looks like *merde* when it
arrives). I ask only once again—

What is a moral life?

## Secret Garden Finale

The sun is going down, later thankfully
as seasons bring what they always have
particularly welcome
now.

We tried to buy the secret garden
more than once, and failed.
Perhaps it isn't possible to buy mythology
or now, we're too old to try.

But, we can sit here. Yes, and admire
feel seasons and terror, in this
season of terror.

# January 2025

Fragmentary.
Not my world, my life.
I can do this—
make the words
make sense.
Not my country
not even the dross.
I can do this—
drive a car
in another country
disoriented, afraid
of the other cars
afraid of the world
crashing into my face.
Afraid of my country
afraid I can't do this
drive
in any country
that of old people
we never expected to be
to enter, or the ruin
of my country.
No better than any
century, millennia, all
the same dross.
Fingernails yellow
even without cigarettes
given up decades ago.
And they have ridges.

No matter, no sense
no words or scream
loud enough.
Leave this earth
old friends, as we must
clinging
to what?

## One Wants There To Be...

...a single story
cradle to grave
corrected by chapters
foolishness, trial and error
something useful
spoken once or evolving
the same dog circling
to find the right spot
sing on key.

> *And my hand still suspended*
> *As if above a letter*
> *I long and dread to close.*

> – Adrienne Rich, "Toward the Solstice"

## …& Tremolos

These lives we live are not linear.
They may go this way and that.
They may go sideways
or one's children may
and never stand.

~

We like hope
because it makes us hopeful.
What do you do
when the smart people say
there is no hope?
And, by the way, we were
the smart people.

~

After his mother died:
"I'm not only the oldest
of my generation
I'm the oldest generation."

~

Now I'm old and for the 1st time in my life
I get up every other morning and exercise
lest like Proust, I never leave my bed
so comfy and abundantly full
of Madeleines.

~

We can't help being ourselves
but, at a certain age
it's a relief to stop trying
not to be.

~

Brown spots on white
white on caramel.
They're of no consequence
except for vanity
telling the world.

~

I am an old woman.
You think it's the same
but it's different. You see
how little life can be worth
yours and everyone else's.
You see everything you
cherished or not, become
more precious or less
for no good reason
diminish and rust.

~

In the time I could have been young
I became old. In the time I could have
mastered the blemishes/foibles/anxieties
of youth, time passed. No hope
of a certain kind of muscle tone
education, reparation, alternative narrative.

~

The cat spoke up.
She spoke loudly
in her soft cat voice.
"I am three." Except
she said "free"
to be cute.

I am seventy-two
*soixante-douze.*
I used to be able
to read and write
and was never cute.
Now, I can only
write; "Will I live
to be seventy-free?"

~

What *will* shut you up?
Wisdom.

~

Unsentimental about his own life
he wept over a soiled and burnt
potholder, and I weep over him
still.

~

How gesture is remembered
obliquely, which means to say
unconsciously without consent:
the way he held a pencil
and put a cup to his lips.
Or, the particular architecture
of Julie's toes.

~

What but grief could be less linear?

~

"Is the patient sick
or not sick?"—Diane Pearl, MD
Is it illness or preoccupation
sensation, mere malaise
world salad, repose
*bien être.*

~

Arthritis—It only hurts
to move it. We don't need
opposable thumbs anyway.

~

Today we celebrate
the body parts
that do not ache:
Not the plantar
not the lumbar
neither toe nor gall.
But, what about tooth
finger, ear, sinus & hip
sorry, sorry planet?
Today we celebrate
because what else
is there to do?

~

The abiding comfort
of a hospital: cheerful, generic care
serious but enlightened community
a weary, ambitious world unto itself.

~

The home health care aid and I
looked at each other quizzically.
The old man shuffled his papers, and said
"It's OK." Afterwards, his wife said
she was surprised, and didn't know.
Let us all not know.

~

*Ring Around the Rosie:*
If the virus doesn't get you
the flood water will.
If the water doesn't get you
the fire will.
If the water puts out the fire
the virus
will get you still.

~

And, no one's counting
because no one's counting.
In our turn
we're supposed to go
young after old
anticipated as the seasons.

~

Some already taken
by Mother Nature & Father Time
The Tooth Fairy, pancreatic cancer
blastic to bone or lytic to bone.
All the thoughts that cannot be
remembered and those stuck
in the head: *rond points & giratoires*
bad marriages & dead pets.

~

If you're dying
you can take myself seriously
because you're really dying.

~

Past lives: glad to be done
sentimental about all of them
good chapters, some
only in retrospect.

~

Retirement is a reward
not a punishment.

~

*Where Do the Memories Go?*
They go out to sea, *nevermore.*
They go to Poe.

~

My friends are both dead
palpably gone, if absence
is palpable.

~

@ Patti Smith's eulogy for Sam Shepard:
To say our names, what we loved
for the last time, and whom.
To say what a generation knew
or thought we could possibly.

~

Old, old age—"Consider the alternative."
Stan used to say, and they all laughed
between complaints.

~

Those childhood friends
you haven't seen for a long time
now look like their parents.

~

The face—Jane Fonda & Madonna
recognizable as someone
with Down's Syndrome.

~

I want to say
I'm no worse for it
but no better.
No
better.

~

You will have forgotten
more than you know
have ever known.
So, what should you keep?

~

Loving the sorrowful
because it's about mortality.
Only mortality makes the universe
exquisite.

~

"I will do my best to stay alive for you
but if I'm unable, you will understand."
—Jay Katz, MD

~

Remembering Yeats
*When you are old and gray.*
Now you are. You didn't want it.
Mortality beckons its ghostly revision.
Tom said, "It's sad, but not a tragedy
when an 85 year old man dies."
There is no measure, no time.
Hide your face
*Amid a crowd of stars.*

# VI
# Gratuit

## THE BAD BOYFRIEND POEMS

Empty-headed broken heart. Volumes
speak the same wail, the same bad boy
bad faith, reincarnated, bad love poem.

What *were* they about?
I'm afraid to look now. The waste
*the wail,* the strange necessity.

A masochistic reparative dance.
The figments that allowed imagination.
Solipsistic wail.

They're in the basement, decaying
for decades, but may come out.
Stay tuned, and watch out!

Lauri Robertson has written poetry for many years
—Adrienne Rich was her mentor. ...& *Tremolos*
is her 7th monograph. She's a psychiatrist and
psychoanalyst, formerly on the clinical faculty of Yale
Medical School, now living in Loire Valley, France.
She is also a fine art photographer, represented on
Nantucket by The Gallery at Four India.

laurirobertson.com

www.ingramcontent.com/pod-product-compliance
Lightning Source LLC
Chambersburg PA
CBHW030311130626
46549CB00002B/809